W9-CPY-017

COMPUTER DECODER

Dorothy Vaughan

COMPUTER SCIENTIST

```
PROGRAM MAIN              SUBROU
INTEGER N, X             INTERGER
EXTERNAL SUB1            EXTERNAL D
X=0                      COMMON /GLO
PRINT *, 61              IF (X. LT.
READ (*,*), N           CALL DUMSUB
CALL SUB1 (X,SUB1)      END
END

REAL*4 N(3), X1(3), X2(3), X3(3
INTEGER*2 PADDING
INTEGER4 NTRI, IUNIT, IRC
CHARACTER (LEN=80) TITLE, FILE
DOUBLE PRECISION,

        CATABLE:: NORMALS (:,
```

ANDI DIEHN

Illustrated by Katie Mazeika

DOROTHY KNEW NUMBERS **MADE SENSE.**
THEY LINED UP JUST RIGHT FOR **ENGINEERING EVENTS!**

WHAT DIDN'T MAKE SENSE, AND MADE **PEOPLE SUFFER,**
WAS HOW PEOPLE WERE DIVIDED **ACCORDING TO COLOR.**

SHE DIDN'T LET THAT STOP HER FROM **BEING THE BEST,**
FROM RISING TO THE TOP AND **HELPING THE REST.**

AND WHEN SHE SAW WHAT A NEW **COMPUTER COULD DO,**
SHE DOVE INTO LEARNING HOW **IT COULD HELP YOU!**

Dorothy Vaughan was a computer during the 1940s and 1950s.

But she wasn't a computer like the computers you might see at school.

Dorothy was a human computer.

She could do math very
quickly and she always
figured out the
right answer,
even if it took a while.

**Numbers made
sense to Dorothy.**

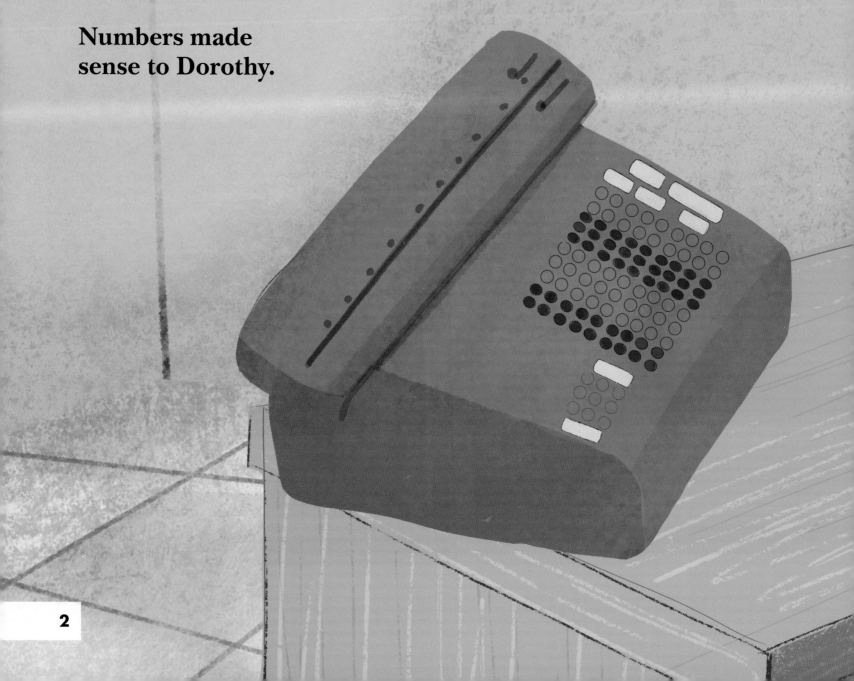

In school, she studied very hard and went to college.

Back then, it was unusual for a woman to go to college. It was even more unusual for an African American woman to go to college.

$5 \times 6 = 30$

$5 \times 7 = 35$

$5 \times 8 = 40$

After college, Dorothy became a math teacher. **Numbers still made sense to Dorothy.**

But she was allowed to teach only African American children.

She didn't earn much money as a teacher. She worried about sending her own children to college.

Dorothy looked for a new job that paid more money.

One day, she spotted a notice on a bulletin board.

The Langley Memorial Aeronautical Laboratory was hiring human computers.

Dorothy applied and got the job!

This was in 1943, during World War II. Many people worked at Langley. This was where engineers tested new airplanes. They figured out how to make the airplanes better at taking off, flying, and landing.

8

The engineers needed people
good at math to help them. These
people were the human computers!

Most of the human computers were women. And most of the engineers were men.

Dorothy loved working as a human computer.
She loved working on solutions to problems.

When World War II ended, the engineers at Langley went to work figuring out how to send people into space! Dorothy was excited to be a part of the team.

At Langley, the numbers made sense. But there was one thing that didn't make sense—segregation.

COLORED ENTRANCE →

Segregation was when black people and white people were forced to stay apart.

At Langley, segregation was the rule. Black people and white people were made to work in different areas.

African American women were on one team of computers and white women were on another team.

17

Dorothy didn't let this stop her. She worked hard. She worked smart. She became the first African American supervisor at Langley!

Dorothy spoke up for equal rights for all people, whether they were black or white. **That made sense to her.**

Langley stopped segrating people when the company became NASA in 1958.

One day, Dorothy felt a strange vibration in the floorboards at Langley. Earthquake? Giant trucks? No!

The shaking was caused by a computer.

Not a human computer. An electronic computer.

The electronic computer worked much faster than a human.

"How can I work with this machine?" Dorothy asked herself.

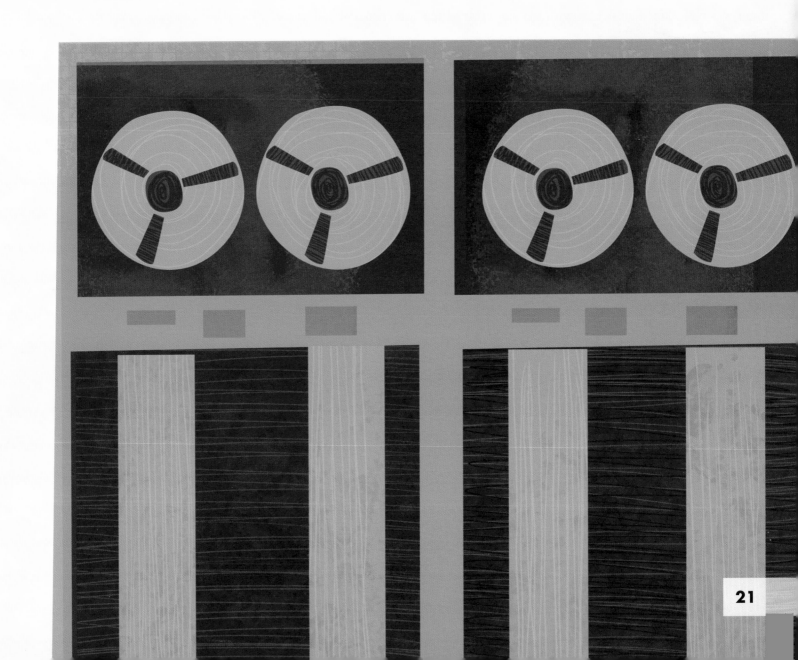

Dorothy decided to learn something new.
This made sense to her.

She went to classes and read books about computers and programming.

Dorothy became an expert at writing computer code.
She helped the other human computers
learn computer code, too.

The work Dorothy did with computers
helped send a man into space!

Dorothy never stopped learning, even
when she was a very old woman.

This just made sense to Dorothy.

Code a Bracelet

Computer coders use numbers and letters to form language that computers understand. You can break your name down into colors to begin to understand how coding works.

What You Need: paper and pencil, string or yarn, several colors of beads

First, spell out your name on a piece of paper.

Then, match each letter in your name to a color of bead.

The letter A might be red,
the letter B might be blue,
R might be green,
and so on.

Put the beads on your string to spell out your name with colors.

The name Barbara would have beads in this order. Now you try!

QUOTE CONNECTIONS!

Try these text-to-text connections!
Can you match the quote to the moment in the story?

"As a college graduate and a teacher, **Dorothy stood near the top** of what most Negro women could hope to achieve."
—Margot Lee Shetterly, *Hidden Figures*

"Forty-eight hours. **I can be ready to go within 48 hours.**"
—Dorothy Vaughan, in an application for a job at Langley

"Reduce your household duties! **Women who are not afraid to roll up their sleeves** and do jobs previously filled by men should call the Langley Memorial Aeronautical Laboratory."
—an employment advertisement in a newspaper, 1940s

"[Working at Langley during the Space Age felt like being on] **the cutting edge of something very exciting.**"
—Dorothy Vaughan

"Effective this date, **Dorothy J. Vaughan**, who has been acting head of the West Area Computers unit, **is hereby appointed head of that unit.**"
—memo sent around Langley in January 1951

TIMELINE

1910 Dorothy Johnson is born on September 20. She later marries Howard Vaughan.

1941 The United States enters World War II.

1943 Dorothy begins working as a human computer at Langley Memorial Aeronautical Laboratory.

1945 World War II ends.

1947 The first electronic computer arrives at Langley Memorial Aeronautical Laboratory.

1949 Dorothy is appointed supervisor of a team of human computers at West Area Computing, a segregated section of Langley.

1954 The U.S. Supreme Court declares school segregation unconstitutional.

Mid 1950s Dorothy learns to program computers because she realizes they are going to be a permanent part of the workplace.

1958 Langley Memorial Aeronautical Laboratory becomes part of NASA and all teams are desegregated, meaning people of all colors work alongside each other and are to be treated the same.

Inside the wind tunnel at Langley

1964 The Civil Rights Act is passed, making discrimination based on race illegal.

1971 Dorothy retires from NASA.

2008 Dorothy dies on November 10.

GLOSSARY

aeronautical: the science of building airplanes and spaceships.

computer code: another name for a computer program.

computer: a device for storing and working with information. Before digital computers, people who worked with numbers were often called human computers.

desegregate: to end segregation.

discrimination: the unfair treatment of a person or a group of people because of who they are.

engineer: someone who uses science, math, and creativity to design and build things.

engineering: the use of science, math, and creativity in the design and construction of things.

NASA: the National Aeronautics and Space Administration, the U.S. organization in charge of space exploration.

permanent: intending to last forever.

programming: to give a computer a set of step-by-step instructions that tells it what to do.

segregation: the policy of keeping people of different races separate from each other.

supervisor: someone who manages the people working on a project.

unconstitutional: going against the U.S. Constitution.

wind tunnel: a tunnel built so airplanes can be safely tested in high winds.

World War II: a war fought between many of the world's nations from 1939 to 1945.